Camp Fraction:
Solving Exciting Word Problems Using Fractions

By
Heidi Lang
& Lisa Allan

Illustrated by
Mike Eustis

Printed in the United States of America.
ISBN-13: 978-1-59363-029-4
ISBN-10: 1-59363-029-8

Prufrock Press, Inc.
P.O. Box 8813
Waco, Texas 76714-8813
(800) 998-2208
Fax (800) 240-0333
http://www.prufrock.com

INTRODUCTION

Really interesting problems based on true facts—as teachers ourselves, we have spent many years looking for such materials for our advanced math students, yet never quite found anything that not only provided an opportunity for applied practice in a math problem solving setting, but was of interest to our students as well. As a result, we chose to create "Camp Fraction."

Every child is inherently interested in the objects present in his or her life, those things used on a daily basis—crayons, paperclips, toothpaste . . . As your students work through the problems in this book, not only will they learn some of the history of any number of things, they will learn lots of fun facts and trivia as well.

At the heart of *Camp Fraction* is the mathematical focus: fractions in a problem-solving format. As your students work through the problems in this book, there will be ample opportunity to add, subtract, multiply, and divide like and unlike fractions, as well as mixed numbers, in meaningful ways. Your students will be expected to generate equivalent fractions, compare fractional quantities, and place fractions in sequential order.

Materials in *Camp Fraction* are intended to be used by advanced learners in grades 4–6, although students in higher grades will benefit as well from applied practice in the area of fractions.

For information on standards addressed in this book, please see page 47.

1/3 + 1/6 = ? , 1/4 + 1/6 = ? , 3/8 + 1/4 = ?

1/10 = 0.1 = 10%
1/2 = 0.5 = 50%
1-1/2 = 1.5 = 150%
1/8 = 0.125 = 12.5%

Camp Fraction
"Where Creativity is Born"
123 Genius Way
Anytown, USA

Welcome Campers!

You will spend the next few weeks discovering more about some of the world's most interesting inventions (while practicing a little math along the way)!

We here at Camp Fraction hope you will soon discover that math goes beyond the walls of your classroom. Math can be found in potato chips, or Silly Putty, or even in your bottle of glue!

Your camp schedule can be found on the next page. We know you'll love doing Arts & Crafts, playing Fun & Games, and exploring our box full of Rainy Day Activities. Bring your appetite for Dinners by the Campfire, and look forward to receiving your first Care Package from Home!

See you soon!

I. Vunder
Director, Camp Fraction

CAMP SCHEDULE

ARTS
&
CRAFTS

Dear Dad,

Did you know that Crayola crayons were invented by two cousins, Edwin Binney and Harold Smith? They worked for a company that used to sell slate pencils for schools. One day they got the idea to make the slate pencils more colorful. The name Crayola comes from the French word "craie" which means chalk, and "oleaginous" which means oily. So a Crayola crayon is just oily chalk! That's what we learned today here at Camp Fraction. Write soon!

Love,
Max

1. The Crayola crayon company employs 2,600 people. If ¼ of those employees called in sick on Monday, how many people would be left to work?

2. The average North American uses 730 crayons by the age of 10. If the average North American kept going at that same rate, how many crayons would he or she use by the age of 25?

3. Most kids spend half an hour per day coloring. If this is true, how many hours per year would an average kid spend coloring?

4. In 1996, the original 8-color box of Crayola crayons was honored when its picture was placed on a 32-cent stamp. At that time, to mail a 1-ounce letter cost 32 cents. If Max wanted to send a 5¼ ounce letter to his parents telling them all the great things he's been learning at Camp Fraction, how much would it cost?

5. In 1903, the cost of an 8-count box of Crayola crayons was 5 cents.

a. If Max had $2.00, what is the greatest number of 8-count boxes of crayons he could buy?

b. What if Max only had ¼ of the $2.00?

Dear Mother,

Glue is awesome! The first glue to receive a patent was made from fish! That was in England in 1750.

Elmer's Glue was invented in 1936 by a chemist named Elmer Pearson who worked for the Borden Company. Elmer is also the name of the bull on the label! It used to come in a glass bottle with a little wooden stick attached to it with a rubber band. When you wanted to use it, you would put the stick in the glue and then slather it on! Write soon!

Love,
Your Little Princess

1. 47 million elementary kids use Elmer's glue on a weekly basis. If ¼ of these kids decided to build a pasta bridge, and each child built one bridge, how many pasta bridges would there be?

2. In one hour, the machine at the glue factory can fill 720 four-ounce bottles of glue. If the machine only had ⅔ of that time, how many four-ounce bottles of glue could it fill?

3. Elmer's Glue was used by a high school student in Rhode Island to build a pasta bridge that held 2,350 pounds. Counselor Clay thinks you can build a bridge that holds 3½ times as many pounds. How many pounds would that be?

4. The average shelf life of a bottle of Elmer's glue is 2 years. Ashley predicted that when she grew up, she would invent a bottle of glue with a shelf life that was 5¼ times that long. Just exactly how long would that be?

Dear Mom and Dad,

It was raining today, so we stayed inside and played with Play-Doh. I made a castle and a rocket. While we were playing we learned that Play-Doh was invented in 1956 by Noah and Joseph McVicker. It was originally only sold in off-white and was first meant to be a wallpaper cleaner. The formula is still top secret!

XXX OOO
Daisy

1. If ⅓ of the 6,000 stores in the U.S. that sell Play-Doh were to suddenly close, how many stores would still be open?

2. Approximately 95,000,000 cans of Play-Doh are manufactured each year. If ¼ of the cans manufactured contain the original off-white color, how many cans would there be that contain a different color?

3. If all of the Play-Doh made since 1956 was squeezed through the Play-Doh Fun Factory, it could make a snake that would wrap around the world 300 times at the equator. The equatorial circumference of the Earth measures 40,076½ kilometers. How many kilometers long would the snake be?

4. On May 13, 2004, Daisy wanted to figure out the weight of ⅛ of all the Play-Doh ever made. She learned that the total amount of Play-Doh produced since 1956 weighs about 700,000,000 pounds. How much would ⅛ of that equal?

5. The following recipe will make enough Play-Doh for one person. Rewrite it to make enough for four people. When you get home, have an adult help you make this recipe for your own Play-Doh:

¼ cup flour   ½ teaspoon cream of tartar
⅛ cup salt   ¼ teaspoon salad oil
¼ cup water

Mix together all ingredients and cook for 3 minutes over low heat, stirring well. Add food coloring if desired.

Dear Mama,

We've been using lots of paper here at Camp Fraction—graph paper, construction paper, and note-book paper! Experts used to think that paper was invented in 105 AD by a Chinese court official named Ts'ai Lun. But now people think the Chinese were making paper as early as 200 BC from old fishing nets. Amazing!

Love,
Ashley

1. The United States uses 90 million short tons of paper each year. A short ton is equal to 2,000 pounds. In $\frac{3}{4}$ of a year, how many pounds of paper are used in the United States?

2. 700 pounds of paper products are used per person each year. If everyone on earth decided to cut back on their paper use, and only $\frac{1}{4}$ of that amount was used, how many pounds of paper products would each person use?

3. There are 500 paper mills currently in operation in the United States. If $\frac{3}{10}$ of the paper mills closed tomorrow, how many would still remain in operation?

4. 41 out of every 100 pieces of trash is paper.

a. If Ashley generated 800 pieces of trash in one day, how many pieces of it would be paper?

b. At this same rate, how many pieces of paper would your class throw away in a school week?

Dear Daddy,

Did you know that rubber bands were invented on March 17, 1845, by a man named Stephen Perry? How long do you think it was before Stephen shot a rubber band at someone?

Hugs,
Chleo

1. The largest rubber band ball was created by Tony Evans from Wales. It weighed 2,524 pounds. If you started saving right now and you could save $315\frac{1}{2}$ pounds per year, how long would it take you to make a rubber band ball as large as Tony's?

2. A typical rubber band can be shot $22\frac{1}{2}$ feet. Aiming for a target 180 feet away, how many shots would you need to take to reach the target?

3a. If a size #16 rubber band weighs $\frac{4}{10,000}$ of a pound, how many #16 rubber bands would you need to collect in order to make a rubber band ball that weighs 10 pounds?

b. If there are 2,500 rubber bands in a box of #16 rubber bands, how many boxes would you need for that 10-pound rubber band ball?

4. Rubber bands are available in a variety of sizes. Here are just a few:

Size 8: $\frac{7}{8}$"   Size 12: $1\frac{3}{4}$"
Size 10: $1\frac{1}{4}$"   Size 16: $2\frac{1}{2}$"
Size 11: $1\frac{1}{2}$"   Size 18:   3"

a. What is the difference in length between a Size 8 and a Size 12 rubber band?

b. What is the difference between a size 10 and a size 11 rubber band?

c. What is the difference between a size 18 and a size 8 rubber band?

Dear Mom and Dad,

You're not going to believe this! Paper clips were patented by Samuel B. Fay in 1867. He made them to attach tickets to fabric, but he thought some people would want to attach two pieces of papers together with them. (I guess he was right!)

The Norwegians claim that Johan Vaaler invented the paper clip. During World War II, when the Germans were occupying Norway, the Norwegian people would wear a paper clip as a symbol of their national unity. Some people were even arrested by the Germans for wearing a paper clip!

Love,
Nikki

1. A standard size paper clip is $1\frac{3}{8}$" long. If a camp cot is 25" wide x $68\frac{1}{2}$" long, how many standard size paper clips would need to be linked together to frame the perimeter of the cot?

2. The longest paper clip chain was $870\frac{1}{4}$ meters long. It was made in 14 hours and 41 minutes by a Swedish student. If the student kept up that same rate and had 88 hours and 6 minutes on his hands, how long would his paper clip chain be?

3. How many billion paper clips are used in the United States each year? Here's a hint: It's $(4\frac{1}{2}$ x 2,000,000,000) + (21,000,000,000 x $\frac{1}{3}$) + ($\frac{1}{4}$ x 8,000,000,000).

4. 35,000,000 paper clips are used each day. A standard paper clip weights 1 gram. How many grams would the number of paper clips used in $3\frac{1}{2}$ days weigh?

Hiya Pops!

We made puppets using felt today, and guess what we found out? The word felt comes from Latin and it means "to beat." No one really knows how felt was invented, but one famous story says that a monk was walking through a desert barefoot. Luckily, he happened to have a camel with him because when the sand got too hot to walk on, the monk tore clumps of the camel's hair off and put them around his feet. After all day of walking and sweating and the hot sun beating on the hair, the monk discovered his special camel's hair shoes had become . . . felt!

xxx 000
Callie

1. Felt costs $8.00 a yard at the Woolly Yak Sewing Shop. Callie is going to wear a dog costume for Halloween. The costume will take 3¼ yards of felt to make. How much money will Callie need to spend at the Woolly Yak?

2. Felt weighs 3⅓ ounces per foot. How much would 6 yards weigh?

3. To make a 20 square inch piece of felt, a felter needs 5 ounces of pure wool. How much wool would be needed to make a piece of felt that is….

   a. 10 square inches?
   b. 5 square inches?
   c. 40 square inches?

4. A 36" x 36" sheet of felt costs $3.99 at the Woolly Yak. Three friends decide to share the cost. How much will each friend need to pay? How many square inches of the felt should each friend get?

RAINY DAY ACTIVITIES

Dear Dad,

You know, a lot of the best inventions were just accidents. That's certainly true with the Slinky. Richard James was really trying to figure out a way to hold up sensitive equipment on ships. He was using springs, and one of them fell on the ground and started "walking." He took it home, showed his wife, and they decided to sell them as toys. His wife picked out the name. In Swedish, Slinky means "stealthy and sleek."

Write soon!
Max

1. The regular price of a Slinky is $3.49 at the Toy Hut. Max decides to buy 6. When he goes to the cashier to pay, he discovers the store is having a sale—$\frac{1}{3}$ off the total sale! How much will Max have to pay for his 6 Slinkys?

2. It takes 87 feet of wire to make a Slinky. Max wants to make a super long Slinky. His plan is to make a Slinky $3\frac{1}{3}$ times the normal size. How much wire will he need to buy?

3. The amount of wire used to make Slinkys in the past 60 years could wrap around the Earth 126 times.

a. If the distance around the Earth is 24,902 miles, how much wire has been used?

b. If Slinkys continue to be produced at the same rate, how much wire will the Slinky company need over the next 15 years?

4. The height of a typical slinky is $2\frac{1}{4}$ inches. If you stacked 25 Slinkys on top of each other, how high would your Slinky stack be?

Dear Mother,

Did you ever hear of Alfred Mosher Butts? The counselors told us about him today. He was an architect who lost his job during the Great Depression. Since he didn't have a job, he started inventing games. He wanted a game that was part luck and part skill. He came up with something we play all the time—Scrabble! It wasn't a hit at first, but then the owner of Macy's Department Stores played it on vacation, loved it, and started selling it in his stores!

Write soon! Love, Your Little Princess

1. There are 6,800 spoken languages in the world. Scrabble is sold in 29 different languages. In how many more languages would Scrabble need to be sold in order for the game to exist in $\frac{1}{4}$ of the world's languages?

2. Scrabble is sold in 121 countries around the world. There are currently 200 identified countries. If the company that produces Scrabble wanted to have their game sold in $\frac{3}{4}$ of the world's countries, in how many more countries would they need to sell their game?

3. There are 100 letter tiles in a game of Scrabble. $\frac{3}{25}$ of the tiles have an "E" on them. How many "E" tiles are there?

4. The highest score you can possibly get in Scrabble in one turn is 1,962 points. (You would have to spell the word "benzoxycamphors" across the bottom of the board!). On a less fortunate day, suppose you create a word worth $\frac{2}{3}$ that amount? What score would you receive?

Dear Mom and Dad,

Did you know the Etch-a-Sketch was developed in the late 1950s by a Frenchman named Arthur Granjean? He called it L'ecran Magique (the magic screen). The reverse side of the screen is coated with aluminum powder.

xxx 000
Daisy

1. The width of a typical Etch-a-Sketch is $9\frac{3}{4}$ inches. If you laid 12 Etch-a-Sketches side by side, how wide would they be?

2. The world's largest Etch-a-Sketch was made by Steve Jacobs of California. He built a large red frame and then laid out 144 standard Etch-a-Sketches inside it. If he had only used $\frac{1}{12}$ of the Etch-a-Sketches, how many would he have needed?

3. There is a pocket sized Etch-a-Sketch that is $4\frac{1}{4}$ inches wide and $3\frac{3}{4}$ inches tall. A travel Etch-a-Sketch is $6\frac{1}{4}$ inches wide and $5\frac{1}{4}$ inches tall.

a. How much wider is the travel version than the pocket version?

b. How much taller?

4. Etch-a-Sketch is sold in $\frac{7}{20}$ of the countries in the world today. If there are 200 countries in existence, how many of them sell Etch-a-Sketches?

Dear Mom,

Guess what I know now? Ole Kirk Christiansen was a carpenter in Denmark who made toys, mostly out of wood. He started a toy company in 1932 called LEGO. The name came from two Danish words that mean "play well." Ole's son started working in the family toy business and in 1958 invented the plastic interlocking blocks we know as LEGOs!

Write soon!

Your favorite daughter,
Ashley

1. There is a prize called the "LEGO Prize" that is awarded each year for exceptional efforts on behalf of children. The award is worth $119,638.18. It would be great to win just $\frac{1}{2}$ of that prize money! How much would that be?

2. Eight robots in the LEGO warehouse can move 660 crates of LEGOs in one hour. If 16 robots were put to work for $2\frac{1}{4}$ hours, how many crates of LEGOs would be moved?

3. On average, each person on the planet Earth has 52 LEGO bricks. An average family in the state of Texas is $3\frac{7}{25}$ people. How many LEGOs does a Texan family likely have?

4. In 1992, the world's largest LEGO castle was built on Swedish TV. It took 40,000 bricks! How many bricks would it take to make a castle $6\frac{1}{4}$ times as large?

Dear Daddy,

I learned something new today. There is a really popular game called Tiddlywinks! Isn't that a great name? After Joseph Assheton Fincher applied for a trademark for his "Tiddledy Winks" in 1889, the game became really popular in the 1890s.

It is played in 2 teams of 2. Each player gets 6 little round chips called "winks" and tries to get them into a pot in the middle of a playing mat using something called a squidger. The points are called "tiddlies"!

How cool is that?

See you soon! I've got to go find a squidger!

Hugs, Chleo

1. The farthest a wink was ever shot was $9\frac{13}{25}$ meters by Ben Stares in 1995. If Ben could flip a wink that distance 5 times in a row, how far would the wink travel in all?

2. Edward Wynn set the record for the fastest Tiddlywinks mile. He flipped a wink a mile in just 52 minutes and 10 seconds. What would $\frac{3}{5}$ of that time be?

3. The farthest distance ever traveled by a Tiddlywink was $2\frac{1}{5}$ miles. The player was put in a "tiddly wagon" and his co-workers moved him along while he winked over and over again! It is 616 miles from Amarillo, Texas, to Houston, Texas. How many times would the player need to set his record in order to travel that distance?

4. The highest a Tiddlywink was ever shot was $11\frac{5}{12}$ feet. The Eiffel Tower is 1,051 feet high.

a. If you could flip a wink 93 times as high as the record height for a Tiddlywink, would it be taller or shorter than the Eiffel Tower?

b. By how much?

Dear Mom and Dad,

I learned lots today! Did you know Silly Putty was invented all because of World War II? It's true! In 1944, the United States had its rubber supplies cut off, but they still needed rubber for truck tires, boots, and other stuff for the war. So the government asked companies to make fake rubber. One guy, James Wright, mixed up some stuff in a tube. It was really gooey, so he threw it on the ground. Boy, was he surprised when it bounced! Cool, huh?

XXX OOO,
Nikki
P.S. Send Silly Putty!

1. More than 300,000,000 eggs of Silly Putty have been sold since 1950! That's about 4,500 tons!

a. If there are 2,000 pounds in a ton, how many pounds of Silly Putty have been sold since 1950?

b. If Binney and Smith produced only $^3/_4$ of that amount, how many pounds of Silly Putty would have been made?

2. Binney and Smith produce about 600 pounds of Silly Putty each day. One day the factory foreman would only allow the machines to operate for $^3/_4$ of a typical day. How many pounds of Silly Putty would be produced in that amount of time?

3. One Silly Putty egg weighs $^{47}/_{100}$ of an ounce.

a. If your mom bought you 500 Silly Putty eggs, how many ounces would they weigh in all?

b. Remember, an ounce is $^1/_{16}$ of a pound. How many pounds would you have with those 500 Silly Putty eggs?

4. The following recipe will make enough fake Silly Putty for four people. Rewrite the recipe for one person! Then, try making your own Silly Putty at home (be sure to ask an adult to help you with this!):

4 oz. white school glue
1 pt. distilled water
1 tsp. borax powder

Hiya Pops!

Did you know that when Mr. Potato Head started out, all kids got in the box were the body parts? They had to supply their own potatoes!! You know what else is cool? Mr. Potato Head was the first toy ever advertised on television!

Love,
Callie

1. Mr. Potato Head sells for $5.99. Callie bought 6 Mr. Potato Heads.

a. How much did she spend?

b. The Toy Hut is having a special sale—$\frac{1}{3}$ off all items. How much will the 6 Mr. Potato Heads cost Callie on sale?

2. Mr. Potato Head weighs $\frac{68}{100}$ pounds. How many Mr. Potato Heads would need to climb on the scale to weigh 17 pounds?

3. In 1974, Mr. Potato Head doubled in size to reach his current height. If he is 7 $\frac{1}{2}$ inches tall, how tall did Mr. Potato Head used to be?

4. 1 out of every 74,293$\frac{3}{4}$ voters in Boise, Idaho wrote in Mr. Potato Head as a candidate for Mayor in 1985. If there are 297,175 registered voters in Boise, how many voted for Mr. Potato Head?

Dear Papa,

I always knew balloons were a blast! Michael Faraday first used balloons in 1824 in his experiments with hydrogen at the Royal Institution in London.

Guess what else? At a college basketball game in Kansas, 1,603 fans popped balloons at the same time! I wish I could have been there!

Love,
Max

1. The largest balloon picture ever made was a mural of the Chicago skyline. The artist used 70,884 balloons. At the Toy Hut, balloons are sold in packages of 25. If Max made a balloon picture with $\frac{1}{3}$ the number of balloons in the record setting picture, how many packages of balloons would Max need to buy?

2. The mural of the Chicago Skyline made of balloons was created at the Hyatt Hotel in Rosemont, Illinois. It measured $17\frac{3}{5}$ by $26\frac{21}{100}$ meters. What was its total area?

3. John Cassiday made 494 balloon sculptures in one hour to set a world record. Continuing at that pace, how many sculptures could John make in $3\frac{1}{2}$ hours?

4. The largest three-dimensional balloon sculpture ever built was of a Diplodocus dinosaur. The sculpture stood $88\frac{1}{2}$ feet tall. A real Diplodocus was 16 feet tall.

a. If you stacked 6 Diplodocuses on top of each other, would they be taller or shorter than the sculpture?

b. By how much?

CARE PACKAGE
FROM HOME

18

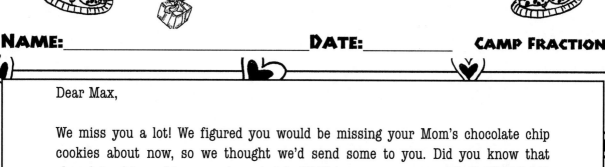

Dear Max,

We miss you a lot! We figured you would be missing your Mom's chocolate chip cookies about now, so we thought we'd send some to you. Did you know that chocolate chip cookies were invented in 1947 by a woman named Ruth Wakefield? It's true! She ran the Toll House Inn in Whitman, Massachusetts. One night she was making Butter Drop Do cookies and decided she would flavor them with some broken up bits of chocolate. She thought the chocolate would melt but was surprised to find that they didn't melt all the way! She decided to call the cookies "Toll House Cookies." Cool, huh?

Love,
Dad

1. One chocolate chip provides enough food energy for an adult to walk 150 feet; 35 chips provides enough food energy to walk a mile; if you ate 875,000 chocolate chips, you would have enough food energy to walk around the world! If you want to get to your cabin, which is 675 feet away, how many chocolate chips should you eat?

2. A typical chocolate chip is usually $1\frac{1}{4}$ centimeters in diameter. One day, Max picked all the chips out of his cookie. He found 55 chips and laid them side by side to form one long chocolate chip line. In centimeters, how long was his line?

3. If you ate 2 cookies per minute, it would take 5,927 years to eat all the Chips Ahoy! cookies made in just one year. If you could only eat $\frac{1}{4}$ of a cookie every minute, how long would it take you?

4. A 12-ounce bag of Nestle semisweet morsels costs $2.59. A recipe calls for 42 ounces of chocolate chips.

a. How many bags of Nestle semisweet morsels will you need to purchase?

b. How many of the bags will you actually use in your recipe?

c. How much money will you need to spend?

My Little Princess,

Did you ever hear of blibber blubber? I hadn't either—until today! It turns out that blibber blubber was the first name for bubble gum!

When bubble gum was first invented, it didn't work very well because it was too sticky. And did you know the reason bubble gum is pink is because that was the only color dye the inventor happened to have?!

Enjoy the gum!

Love,
Mother

1. The largest bubble gum bubble ever blown was $58^2/_5$ centimeters by Susan Montgomery Williams in 1994. Is that greater than, less than, or equal to…

a. $58^4/_{10}$ centimeters?
b. $58^3/_4$ centimeters?
c. $58^1/_3$ centimeters?

2. The longest gum wrapper chain was 10,387 meters. It used 792,691 wrappers! To make a chain $3^1/_2$ times longer, how many wrappers would you need?

3. The average American chews 183 sticks of gum each year. How much gum would the average American chew in 3 years and 4 months?

4. The Wrigley's company has machines at their factory that wrap gum and put it into packages. Each machine has 6,000 moving parts. If $^2/_3$ of those parts stopped working, how many parts would still be functioning?

Dear Daisy,

We saw this PEZ dispenser at the store and thought of you—we know you like tipping the little heads back on these things and getting the candy bricks that come out of their necks!

Hard to believe that PEZ dispensers have been around so long—since 1927, in fact. A man from Vienna, Austria, named Eduard Haas invented them as a way to help people stop smoking. Instead of a cigarette, he hoped people would reach for a peppermint candy from his little dispenser. The word PEZ even comes from the word peppermint. You see, in German the word for peppermint is "pfefferminz." If you take the first letter of pfefferminz, P, then the middle letter, E, and the last letter, Z, you have PEZ!

Love,
Mom and Dad

1. The candies put into PEZ dispensers are called bricks. There are 12 bricks in a package of PEZ. $\frac{1}{4}$ of the bricks are flavored orange. Daisy's parents sent her 30 packs of PEZ candy. How many orange bricks will she be able to share with her cabin mates?

2. The most expensive PEZ dispenser ever sold was called an Advertising Regular. It didn't have a head, like a lot of PEZ dispensers, and it had a company's advertisement on the side. It sold for $\frac{1}{5}$ of $21,875. How much did it cost?

3. There are four different PEZ dispensers that are considered the tallest: Bugs Bunny, Yosemite Sam, Uncle Sam, and the Knight are all $4\frac{7}{8}$ inches tall. If you stacked all four of these dispensers on top of each other, how high would they reach?

4. The widest PEZ dispenser you can buy looks like Thor, the Norse god of Thunder. Thor is $2\frac{3}{8}$ inches wide.

a. If Daisy had a shelf 14 inches wide, could she display all 6 of her Thor dispensers?

b. Why or why not?

Dear Ashley,

I thought you might be needing some extra toothpaste right about now! Are you brushing your teeth? I thought you might be interested to know that toothpaste was first used in China and India in 500 B.C.! Before people used toothpaste, they would clean their teeth using crushed eggshells or the burnt hooves of animals. Yuck!

Love,
Mama

1. Toothpaste is an abrasive. It grinds away the food and plaque on your teeth. In a typical tube of toothpaste, $^3/_{15}$ of the tube is filled with abrasive. How many fifths of a tube of toothpaste are not filled with abrasive?

2. The oldest written formula for toothpaste is this one from Ancient Egypt. It was written in the 4th century A.D.:

   $^1/_{100}$ ounce rock salt
   $^1/_{50}$ ounce mint
   $^1/_{100}$ ounce dried iris flower
   20 grains pepper

   This formula will create enough toothpaste for one person to brush his teeth. You need to make enough toothpaste for the entire village of 400 people. How would you rewrite the formula?

3. $1,800,000,000 is spent each year on toothpaste. What would $^1/_3$ of that be?

4. One drum of mint oil weighs 400 pounds. One drum can flavor 400,000 tubes of toothpaste. Given $5^1/_4$ drums of mint oil, how many tubes of toothpaste could get that minty fresh feeling?

Dear Chleo,

I bet your toothbrush is worn out from all the brushing you've been doing, so I'm sending you a new one. And be glad for it, because once upon a time, toothbrushes used bristles made from the necks of pigs!

Toothbrushes were first mass produced in America in 1885, but most people didn't brush their teeth until after World War II when soldiers brought the habit home with them from the army!

Love,
Daddy

1. $^{13}/_{100}$ people brush their teeth from side to side, while the rest brush from top to bottom. If 400 people were brushing their teeth, how many would you expect to see brushing from top to bottom?

2. People spent $692,000,000 on toothbrushes in 1998. If all the toothbrushes had been on sale for $^1/_4$ off, how much money would have been spent?

3. Rows of toothbrush bristles are made up of "tufts." Typical tufted brushes are 6 tufts long and 3 tufts wide.

a. How many total tufts are found on a typical toothbrush?

b. Some brushes have 28 tufts. How many times larger is that than a typical brush?

4. Dentists recommend changing your toothbrush every 3 months. If Chleo followed her dentist's advice, how many toothbrushes would she need from the time she turned 2 until she turned 10¾ years old?

Dear Nikki,

In the southwestern United States, archaeologists found some petrified cakes with holes in the center of them while they were digging in some prehistoric ruins. We hope these doughnuts are a little fresher!

In the 1800s, the Dutch made "olykoeks" or "oily cakes" as special treats. They were filled with apples, prunes, or raisins. Then, in 1847 a woman named Elizabeth Gregory added some nutmeg to her olykoeks and filled the center with nuts. She also gave them a special name—doughnuts!

Enjoy!
XXX OOO
Mom and Dad

1. Winchell's House of Donuts once made a donut that weighed 500 pounds and stood 95 feet in diameter. If the donut were sliced into twelfths, how many pounds would $^7/_{12}$ of the donut weigh?

2. The record for the most jelly donuts eaten in 3 minutes without licking the lips is 6. If the record setter could continue at this pace, how long would it take to eat 26 donuts?

3. The largest jelly donut weighed 3,739 pounds. It was 16 feet in diameter and 16 inches tall. Nikki decided to break this record. She made a donut, but forgot to put in the yeast, so her donut ended up a little flat. In fact, its height was only $^1/_5$ of the record setter's height. How tall was Nikki's donut?

4. A typical Krispy Kreme Donut Shop can make 125 donuts in $^1/_4$ minute. How many donuts can be made in one hour?

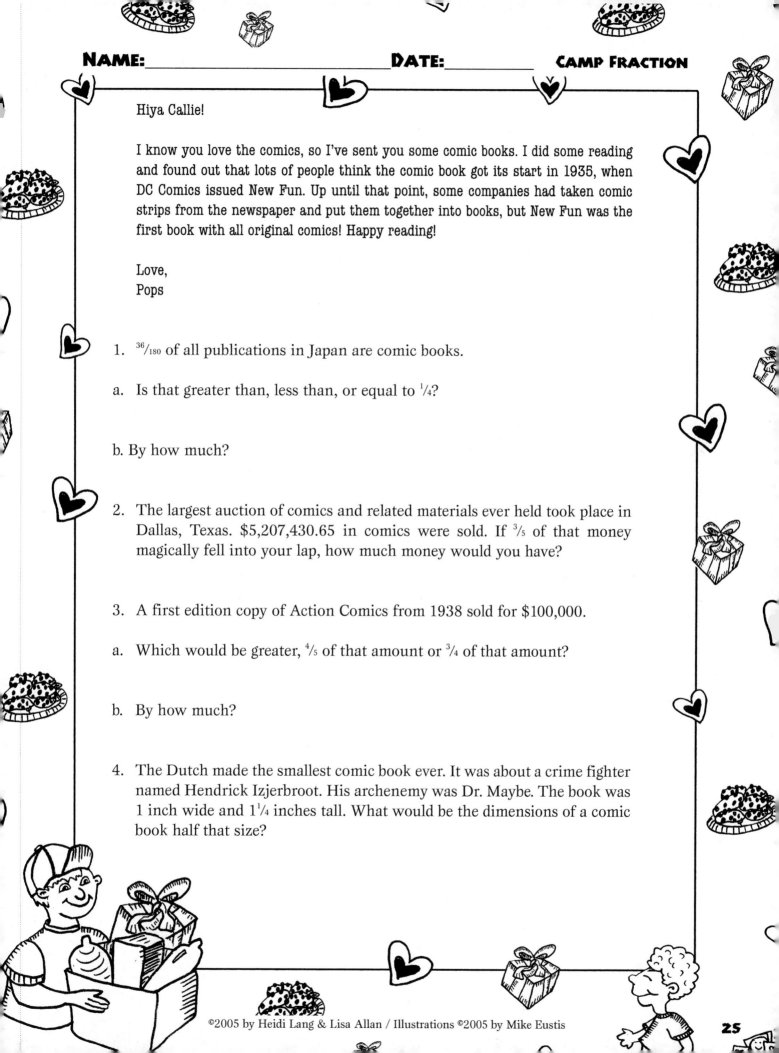

Hiya Callie!

I know you love the comics, so I've sent you some comic books. I did some reading and found out that lots of people think the comic book got its start in 1935, when DC Comics issued New Fun. Up until that point, some companies had taken comic strips from the newspaper and put them together into books, but New Fun was the first book with all original comics! Happy reading!

Love,
Pops

1. $^{36}/_{180}$ of all publications in Japan are comic books.

a. Is that greater than, less than, or equal to $^1/_4$?

b. By how much?

2. The largest auction of comics and related materials ever held took place in Dallas, Texas. $5,207,430.65 in comics were sold. If $^3/_5$ of that money magically fell into your lap, how much money would you have?

3. A first edition copy of Action Comics from 1938 sold for $100,000.

a. Which would be greater, $^4/_5$ of that amount or $^3/_4$ of that amount?

b. By how much?

4. The Dutch made the smallest comic book ever. It was about a crime fighter named Hendrick Izjerbroot. His archenemy was Dr. Maybe. The book was 1 inch wide and $1^1/_4$ inches tall. What would be the dimensions of a comic book half that size?

FUN & GAMES

Dear Dad,

Today the counselors played Frisbee with us. They told us that during the Great Depression kids used to play with metal pie plates because they didn't have a lot of money. Some of the plates were made by the "Frisbie" pie company. When the metal plates started flying, the kids would yell "Frisbie!" to warn others because the metal could hurt them with its sharp edges.

In 1948, two guys named Walter Frederick Morrison and Warren Franscioni made plastic ones they called "Flyin' Saucers." When the Wham-O company started making them, they liked the sound of "frisbie" so they changed the name. Neat!

See you soon! Max

1. Classic Frisbees come in three colors: lime-green, purple, and orange. The classic Frisbee weighs 90 grams. Max bought one of each color.

a. How many grams did they weigh in all?

b. What would $\frac{1}{4}$ of that weight be?

2. In 1998, the Men's Distance world record for throwing a Frisbee was set by Scott Stokely. He was able to send a Frisbee flying for $693\frac{3}{10}$ feet. If Scott could throw a Frisbee that same distance three times in a row, how far would the Frisbee travel?

3. In 1968, the United States Navy spent about $400,000 to test Frisbees as vehicles for keeping flares aloft. Max's parents spent about $\frac{1}{50}$ of that amount to send him to Camp Fraction for the month of July. How much did Max's parents spend?

4. In 1994, Anna Kreml threw a Frisbee $447\frac{1}{5}$ feet, setting the Women's Distance Record. Determine whether the following distances are greater than, less than, or equal to her record.

a. $447\frac{2}{10}$ feet _____ $447\frac{1}{5}$ feet

b. $447\frac{4}{5}$ feet _____ $447\frac{1}{5}$ feet

c. $447\frac{1}{4}$ feet _____ $447\frac{1}{5}$ feet

Dear Mother,

It was windy here today, so the counselors helped us make kites! It was so fun! They also told us that the earliest written account of anyone flying a kite was in the year 200 BC! That's right! A Chinese general named Han Hsin flew a kite over the walls of a city he wanted to attack. It helped him measure how far his army would need to tunnel to get past the defenses of the city!

Love,
Your Little Princess

1. The smallest kite ever flown was $\frac{4}{100}$ inch x $\frac{3}{100}$ inch It was flown in Washington State by Nobuhiko Yoshizuni. If the kite had been 10 times its original size, what would its dimensions have been?

2. In 1898, a box kite flew more than two miles above the Earth. It reached a height that was $\frac{3}{4}$ of 16,628 feet. How high would that be?

3. The world's largest kite, the MegaRay, took 500 hours to design and build. It was 38 x 66 meters. If the designers could have created the MegaRay in $\frac{7}{10}$ of the time, how long would it have taken?

4. On April 4, 1976, Kazuuhiko Asaba Kamakura flew 1050 kites on a single line! If the line was only $\frac{2}{3}$ the length of Kazuuhiko's line, how many kites would he have been able to fly?

Dear Mom and Dad,

I've been riding bikes almost all of my life and I never knew anything about them until today! Did you know that they were invented in 1791 by a frenchman named Comte Mede de Sivrac? The first bicycle wasn't really a bicycle because it didn't have any pedals. Instead, you pushed it with your feet—like a skateboard!

It wasn't until 1839 that Kirkpatrick MacMillan added pedals. And people thought he was crazy! But I guess history has shown he wasn't crazy at all.

Your crazy little girl,
Daisy

1. The largest bicycle in the world is called "Frankencycle" and it is $11^{1}/_{12}$ feet high. Daisy is 4 feet 4 inches tall. How much taller is Frankencycle?

2. The fastest anyone has ever gone on a bicycle is $167^{43}/_{1000}$ miles per hour. This was achieved by a man named Fred Rompelberg. If Fred maintained that speed for five hours, how many miles would he have traveled?

3. The smallest bicycle ever built had a front wheel that was only $^{43}/_{100}$ inches in diameter. It was ridden a distance of 16 feet! How much larger would the front wheel need to be in order to measure $^{1}/_{2}$ inch in diameter?

4. A team of 32 divers once pedaled a tricycle $116^{66}/_{100}$ miles under water. It took them 75 hours 20 minutes. If the divers had the energy, and another 301 hours and 20 minutes, pedaling at the same speed, how far might they travel?

Dear Mama,

There is a legend that says an American man named George Hansburg was traveling in Burma when he met a poor farm girl named Pogo. She really wanted to go to her temple to pray every day, but she didn't have any shoes and the ground was very rocky so her father made a jumping stick on which she could ride to the temple. When Mr. Hansburg went home, he attached a spring to the jumping stick design, called it a Pogo Stick, and started selling! I'm not sure how much of that story I believe, but a man named Mr. Hansburg DID get a patent for a Pogo Stick in 1919. Decide for yourself!!

Your favorite daughter,
Ashley

1. The person who set the world record for continuous jumping on a Pogo Stick jumped for $\frac{1}{4}$ of an hour 164 different times. How many total hours did he jump?

2. Ashrita Furman has gone a greater distance on a Pogo Stick than any other person. He traveled $123^{11}/_{100}$ miles on his Pogo Stick in 12 hours 27 minutes. If he could continue at that same pace, how far could he go in 87 hours 9 minutes?

3. Ashrita also set a record by climbing all 1,899 steps at the CN Tower in Ontario, Canada, in 57 minutes 51 seconds. If Ashrita jumped at an even pace, how many steps would he have climbed in 19 minutes 17 seconds?

4. A Razor Go-Go Pogo Stick costs $98.50. It is $44\frac{1}{2}$ inches tall. A Razor Go-Go Jr. is $36\frac{1}{2}$ inches tall and costs $69.50.

a. If you laid 10 Razor Go-Gos and 10 Razor Go-Go Jr.s end to end, how long would the line be?

b. How much would this cost?

Dear Daddy,

We had so much fun playing badminton today! It was a blast trying to get the "birdie" over the net by hitting it with our rackets. In some way or another, badminton has been around for 2,000 years. It was played in ancient Greece, China, and India. It became popular in England in the 1800s. The Duke of Beaufort played it all the time at his house. And guess what?! His house was called Badminton House! That's why we call the game badminton!

Hugs,
Chleo

1. Badminton rackets weigh $4\frac{1}{2}$ ounces. If Chleo bought a box that held 10 rackets, how much did the box weigh?

2. Birdies average 76 grains (a grain is $\frac{1}{5760}$ of a pound). Each birdie has 14–16 feathers fixed in a cork. What is the greatest number of birdies you could put on a scale without going over one pound in weight?

3. The feathers are $2\frac{1}{2}$ inches to $2\frac{3}{4}$ inches in length from their tip to the top of the cork base. Chleo found a birdie with 16 feathers. Half of them were $2\frac{1}{2}$ inches long, the other half were $2\frac{3}{4}$ inches long. If she laid the feathers end to end, how long would the line of feathers be?

4. The longest badminton match ever was $20\frac{2}{3}$ times as long as the shortest badminton match ever. The shortest match took 6 minutes to play. How long did it take to play the longest match ever?

Dear Mom and Dad,

We went roller skating today. It was so fun! There was a man in Holland in the early 1700s who decided he wanted to go ice skating on dry land so he nailed wooden spools to strips of wood and attached the wood to his shoes. He called his creation "Skeelers." What's really weird is they have a picture of the man, but nobody knows his name!

Love,
Nikki

1. Did you know that $7/10$ of all Americans have attended a birthday party at a skating center? In a room of 300 people, how many are likely to have done so?

2. A sports promoter named Leo Seltzer came up with the idea of something called a Roller Derby. Twenty-five teams of 2 had to skate 3,000 miles around a track. That's like skating from San Diego, California, to New York City! The winner was the team that completed it in the shortest time. If the track was $1/4$ mile long, how many laps would the skaters need to make?

3. In the Roller Derby, one team member had to be moving at all times during the $11\frac{1}{2}$ hour session each day. When team members weren't moving, they slept on cots in the middle of the skating rink. The Roller Derby started on August 13, 1935. Teammates Clarice Martin and Bennie McKay won on September 22 of the same year. If they skated $11\frac{1}{2}$ hours each day, how many hours did they skate in all?

4. Not all of the teams finished the Roller Derby. In fact, only $36/100$ of the teams completed the long trek. There were only 25 teams participating. How many did not complete the Roller Derby?

Dear Papa,

Just thought you might want to know that some form of hula hoops have been around since ancient times, but they weren't always made of plastic. They used to be made of bamboo, or wood, or vines! Richard Knerr and Arthur "Spud" Melin, the founders of the Wham-O company, decided to make them plastic. Groovy!

Max

1. The most Hula Hoops ever to be spun at the same time was 83. This amazing record was set by Cia Granger of Finland, who was able to keep them spinning for three full revolutions!

a. Max decided he was going to break Cia's record by keeping 6 times as many Hula Hoops spinning. How many Hula Hoops will Max need?

b. Oops! Max couldn't even get all those Hula Hoops on his body. He decided he better cut back, using only $\frac{1}{3}$ of the Hula Hoops in his original goal. How many would that be?

2. How many Hula Hoops were sold in the first 6 months of production? Here's a hint: the answer is $\frac{4}{7}$ of 35,000,000.

3. Hula Hoops originally sold for $1.98.

a. Using the answer you obtained in question number two, determine how much money was spent on Hula Hoops in the first 6 months.

b. Then determine what $\frac{2}{3}$ of that amount would be.

4. Currently, $12\frac{1}{2}$ million Hula Hoops are sold every $\frac{1}{12}$ of a year. How many are sold in two years?

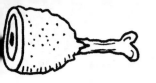

DINNER
BY THE
CAMPFIRE

Dear Dad,

When you went to Germany did you eat a hot dog? I'm only asking because it was German immigrants who first brought hot dogs to America! When the German immigrants came to New York City in the 1860s, they sold hot dogs from carts. Pretty soon someone realized that if you put the hot dog in a bun it made it easier to carry.

Love,
Max

1. The longest hot dog ever made was $6\frac{9}{10}$ meters long. It was made in Radford, Virginia, in 2002. How long would the hot dog have been if it were only $\frac{2}{3}$ that length?

2. Out of every 100 adults, $87\frac{6}{10}$ prefer mustard as a topping on their hot dogs. If 500 adults came for a cookout at your house, how many would likely put mustard on their hot dogs?

3. Baseball legend Babe Ruth once ate 12 hot dogs and 8 bottles of soda between games of a doubleheader. After the game, he was rushed to the hospital with bad indigestion. Perhaps if he had only eaten $\frac{2}{3}$ of the hot dogs and $\frac{1}{4}$ of the soda he would have been fine. How many hot dogs and how much soda would that be?

4. The average hot dog takes $6\frac{1}{10}$ bites to eat. At the Camp Fraction hot dog eating contest, Max ate 12 hot dogs. How many bites did he take?

Dear Mother,

Mmmm, mmmm! I love Kool-Aid! We should definitely drink it more at home! Did you know Kool-Aid is the official state drink of Nebraska?! That's because the man who invented it, Edwin Perkins, was from Nebraska. Edwin had a job selling a drink mix called "Fruit Smack" by mail. Unfortunately for him, the mix was a liquid in a little bottle and it kept breaking. That's why he decided to invent a powdered drink mix. I, for one, am grateful!

Your Little Princess

1. An 8-quart can of Kool-Aid costs $3.50. If you had $33.25, how many quarts of Kool-Aid could you purchase?

2. 17 gallons of Kool-Aid are consumed every second during the summer! In $2\frac{1}{2}$ minutes, how much Kool-Aid is consumed?

3. If all the envelopes of Kool-Aid sold in a year were laid end to end, they would stretch 58,524 miles. How far would $\frac{2}{3}$ of the Kool-Aid envelopes sold in a year stretch?

4. The shelf life of an unopened package of Kool-Aid is $\frac{120}{5}$ months. Mother discovered a packet of Kool-Aid at the very back of the kitchen cupboard. By checking the expiration date, she found that the Kool-Aid was 1 year, 10 months old.

a. Should she drink it?

b. Why or why not?

Dear Mom and Dad,

The Ancient Egyptians thought of just about everything—including marshmallows! They used to make a candy out of honey and it was thickened with the sap from the root of a plant that grew in the marshes—the Marsh Mallow plant!

And guess what else? Marshmallows are sometimes used to lure alligators out of swamps!

Love,
Daisy

1. The farthest a marshmallow was ever blown out of one nostril and caught in the mouth of a catcher was $4^{96}/_{100}$ meters. What would 50 times that distance be? (P.S. The catcher ate the marshmallow!)

2. 15,000,000 pounds of Jet Puffed marshmallows are purchased in $^1/_6$ of a year. How many are purchased in a year?

3. It took 27 hours to make one Marshmallow Peep in 1953. Today it only takes $^1/_{270}$ of that time. How many minutes does it take to make a Peep now?

4. The eyes on Marshmallow Peeps used to be hand painted, but now they are painted by machines that can paint 3,800 Peeps' eyes per minute. How many Peeps' eyes can be painted in $^3/_4$ of a minute?

Dear Mama,

At dinner tonight, I put tons of ketchup on my hot dog. The counselor started telling me some amazing stuff about ketchup. Did you know that it was first brought back to Europe from China in the 1600s by sailors? In China it was called "ketsiap" and was a salty pickled fish sauce. Once it got back to Europe, people started making all kinds of variations. In 1821, the first tomato ketchup was made. It was called "love apple" ketchup.

Your favorite daughter,
Ashley

P.S. President Nixon used to put ketchup on his cottage cheese!

1. How many US households own a bottle of ketchup? The answer: $\frac{1}{4}$ of $3\frac{22}{25}$. How many would that be?

2. $\frac{3}{5}$ of all bottles of ketchup are sold outside the United States. Out of 600 bottles, how many are sold in the US?

3. Ketchup travels at a rate of 25 miles every year. How many miles could ketchup go in 73 days?

4. Dustin Phillips of Los Angeles, California, once drank 91% of a 14-ounce bottle of ketchup through a $\frac{1}{4}$-inch straw in 33 seconds. How many ounces of ketchup did Dustin drink?

Dear Daddy,

Like so many things, mustard has been around for a long, long time. The ancient Egyptians used to pop mustard seeds into their mouth. Ancient Greeks added the seeds to stews. The Ancient Romans crushed the seeds and mixed them with wine to make a paste that is like our mustard today. A lady named Mrs. Clements from England gets all the credit for inventing a powder of mustard. Cool thing you should know—in Denmark and India people sometimes spread mustard seeds around the outside of their homes to keep out evil spirits!

Hugs,
Chleo

1. $^{69}/_{100}$ of American households buy a jar of mustard each year. If you visited 400 houses in the United States and looked into their refrigerators, how many jars of mustard would you likely see?

2. Mustard will last for 12 months if it is in a squeeze bottle. It will last $1\frac{1}{2}$ times longer in a glass bottle. How long would that be?

3. It takes $\frac{1}{4}$ teaspoon of crushed mustard seeds mixed with a liquid like water, vinegar, beer, or wine to make $\frac{1}{2}$ teaspoon of prepared mustard. There are 5 teaspoons of prepared mustard left in the jar on the counter. How many teaspoons of crushed mustard seeds were needed to make that prepared mustard?

4. A 20-ounce squeeze bottle of French's mustard contains approximately 120 servings. There are $\frac{1}{2}$ that many campers at Camp Fraction. Camp Fraction went through $4\frac{2}{3}$ bottles of mustard in one week. How many servings is that per camper?

5. One teaspoon of Colman's Dry Mustard contains $\frac{1}{2}$ gram of fat. Steve makes his famous pretzel dip that uses $3\frac{1}{2}$ teaspoons of Colman's Dry Mustard. How many grams of fat are in the dip?

Dear Mom and Dad,

Did you know that the potato chip was invented by a man named George Crum? It's true! In 1853, George Crum was a chef at Moon Lake Lodge in Saratoga Springs, NY. One day a guest told Chef Crum the french fries he made were too thick so he cut the potatoes really, really thin just to be mean! But the guest liked them! So did everybody else, and the potato chip was born!

Love,
Nikki

1. The average potato chip is $^6/_{10}$ of an inch thick.

a. If you were able to stack 390 potato chips one on top of the other, how many inches tall would this stack be?

b. How many feet tall?

2. In $^1/_2$ an hour a factory can produce 1,750 pounds of potato chips.
a. How many pounds could they produce in $^1/_4$ of an hour?

b. How many in 2 hours?

3a. Ridged chips are $^{210}/_{1000}$ of an inch thick. Write this fraction as a decimal.

b. If you stacked 50 ridged chips on top of each other, how many inches tall would the stack be?

4. The world's largest potato chip was produced by the Pringle's Company in 1990. It measured 23 inches wide and 14 $^1/_2$ inches long.

a. If you laid 10 identical chips end to end lengthwise, how long would this row of chips be?

b. You come across another row of these identical chips that measure 43$^1/_2$ feet long. How many potato chips are in this row?

5. The average person eats the equivalent of 96 one-ounce bags of potato chips each year. An ounce is $^1/_{16}$ of a pound. How many pounds does the average person eat each year?

40

Hiya Pops!

We had the best time last night! We had dinner by the campfire and got to eat Popsicles for dessert. They were yummy! Counselor Steve said that Popsicles were once called Epsicles! That's because the person who invented them was Frank Epperson. He was 11 years old when he left a mixed up soda drink with a straw in it on his porch in the cold overnight. When he went out in the morning he pulled the frozen drink out with the straw and had a special morning treat!

XXX OOO
Callie

1. In $\frac{3}{4}$ of a year, 750,000 Popsicles are sold in the United States. How many are sold in 1 year's time?

2. There are typically 30 flavors of Popsicles available at any time, but the most popular flavor is orange. The Ice Cream Shack is holding a Popsicle contest to invent new flavors. Callie creates $2\frac{5}{6}$ times the typical number of flavors. How many new flavors does Callie come up with?

3. Each Popsicle weighs $1\frac{3}{4}$ ounces. How much would a box of 12 Popsicles weigh?

4. National Cherry Popsicle Day falls on August 26th each year. Callie is going to throw a special party for 484 of her closest friends. Each box of Popsicles has 12 Popsicles in it, but only $\frac{1}{3}$ of them are cherry flavored. Callie wants to buy enough boxes so that every one of her friends can have a cherry Popsicle. How many boxes will she need to buy?

CAMP FRACTION ANSWER KEY

ARTS & CRAFTS

page 2: Crayons
1. 1,950 people
2. 1,825 crayons
3. 182½ hours
4. $1.68
5. a. 40 boxes; b. 10 boxes

page 3: Glue
1. 11,750,000 bridges
2. 480 bottles
3. 8,225 pounds
4. 10½ years

page 4: Play-Doh
1. 4,000 stores
2. 71,250,000 cans
3. 12,022,950 kilometers
4. 87,500,000 pounds
5. 1 cup flour, 2 teaspoons cream of tartar, ½ cup salt, 1 teaspoon salad oil, 1 cup water

page 5: Paper
1. 135,000,000,000 pounds
2. 175 pounds
3. 350 mills
4. a. 328 pieces of paper; b. 1,640 pieces of paper per school week

page 6: Rubber Bands
1. 8 years
2. 8 shots
3. a. 25,000 rubber bands; b. 10 boxes
4. a. ⅞ inch; b. ¼ inch; c. 2⅛ inches

page 7: Paper Clips
1. 136 paper clips

2. 5,221½ meters
3. 18,000,000,000 paper clips
4. 122,500,000 grams

page 8: Felt
1. $26.00
2. 60 ounces
3. a. 2½ ounces; b. 1¼ ounces; c. 10 ounces
4. a. $1.33; b. 432 square inches

RAINY DAY ACTIVITIES

page 10: Slinky
1. $13.96
2. 290 feet
3. a. 3,137,652 miles; b. 784,413 miles
4. 56¼ inches

page 11: Scrabble
1. 1,671 languages
2. 29 countries
3. 12 "E" tiles
4. 1,308 points

page 12: Etch-a-Sketch
1. 117 inches
2. 12 Etch-a-Sketches
3. a. 2 inches; b. 1½ inches
4. 70 countries

page 13: LEGOs
1. $59,819.09
2. 2,970 crates
3. 170¹⁴/₂₅ LEGOs
4. 250,000 bricks

page 14: Tiddlywinks
1. $47^3/_5$ meters
2. 31 minutes, 18 seconds
3. 280 times
4. a. taller; b. $10^3/_4$ feet

page 15: Silly Putty
1. a. 9,000,000 pounds;
b. 6,750,000 pounds
2. 450 pounds
3. a. 235 ounces; b. 14
pounds, 11 ounces
4. 1 ounce white school glue,
$^1/_4$ pint distilled water, $^1/_4$
teaspoon borax powder

page 16: Mr. Potato Head
1. a. $35.94; b. $23.96
2. 25 potato heads
3. $3^3/_4$ inches
4. 4 voters

page 17: Balloons
1. 946 packages
2. $461^{37}/_{125}$ square meters
3. 1,729 sculptures
4. a. taller; b. $7^1/_2$ feet

CARE PACKAGE FROM HOME

page 19: Chocolate Chip Cookies
1. $4^1/_2$ chips
2. $68^3/_4$ centimeters
3. 47,416 years
4. a. 4 bags; b. $3^1/_2$ bags;
c. $10.36

page 20: Bubble Gum
1. a. equal to; b. less than; c.
greater than
2. $2,774,418^1/_2$ wrappers

3. 610 sticks of gum
4. 2,000 parts

page 21: PEZ Dispensers
1. 90 orange bricks
2. $4,375
3. $19^1/_2$ inches
4. a. No; b. It would be $^1/_4$
inch too short.

page 22: Toothpaste
1. $^4/_5$ of the tube
2. 4 oz. rock salt, 8 oz. mint,
4 oz. dried iris, 3. 8,000
pepper grains
3. $600,000,000
4. 2,100,000 tubes

page 23: Toothbrush
1. 348 people
2. $519,000,000
3. a. 18 tufts; b. $1^5/_9$
4. 35 toothbrushes

page 24: Doughnuts
1. $291^2/_3$ pounds
2. 13 minutes
3. $3^1/_5$ inches
4. 30,000 donuts

page 25: Comic Books
1. a. less than b. $^1/_{20}$
2. $3,124,458.39
3. a. $^4/_5$; b. $5,000
4. $^1/_2$ inch x $^5/_8$ inch

FUN & GAMES

page 27: Frisbee
1. a. 270 grams; b. $67^1/_2$
grams
2. $2,079^9/_{10}$ feet
3. $8,000

CAMP FRACTION ANSWER KEY

4. a. equal to; b. less than; c. less than

page 28: Kites
1. $^4/_{10}$ inch x $^3/_{10}$ inch
2. 12,471 feet
3. 350 hours
4. 700 kites

page 29: Bicycle
1. $6^3/_4$ feet
2. $835^{43}/_{200}$ miles
3. $^7/_{100}$ inches
4. $466^{16}/_{25}$ miles

page 30: Pogo Sticks
1. 41 hours
2. $861^{77}/_{100}$ miles
3. 633 steps
4. a. $67^1/_2$ feet; b. $1,680

page 31: Badminton
1. 45 ounces
2. 75 birdies
3. 42 inches
4. 2 hours 4 minutes

page 32: Roller Skates
1. 210 people
2. 12,000 laps
3. $471^1/_2$ hours
4. 16 teams

page 33: Hula Hoops
1. a. 498 Hula Hoops; b. 166 Hula Hoops
2. 20,000,000 Hula Hoops
3. a. $39,600,000;
b. $26,400,000
4. 300,000,000 Hula Hoops

DINNER BY THE CAMPFIRE

page 35: Hot Dogs
1. $4^3/_5$ meters
2. 438 adults
3. 8 hot dogs, 2 bottles of soda
4. $73^1/_5$ bites

page 36: Kool-Aid
1. 76 quarts
2. 2,550 gallons
3. 39,016 miles
4. a. Yes; b. It won't go bad for another two months.

page 37: Marshmallows
1. 248 meters
2. 90,000,000 pounds
3. 6 minutes
4. 2,850 eyes

page 38: Ketchup
1. $^{97}/_{100}$ households
2. 240 bottles
3. 5 miles
4. $12^{37}/_{50}$ ounces

page 39: Mustard
1. 276 households
2. 18 months
3. $2^1/_2$ teaspoons
4. $9^1/_3$ servings
5. $1^3/_4$ grams

page 40: Potato Chips
1. a. 234 inches; b. $19^1/_2$ feet
2. a. 875 potato chips;
b. 7000 potato chips
3. a. 0.210; b. $10^1/_2$ inches
4. a. 145 inches; b. 36 potato chips
5. 6 pounds

page 41: Popsicles
1. 1 million
2. 85 flavors
3. 21 ounces
4. 121 boxes

Standards

The activities in this book address many of the essential skills and knowledge contained in the Texas Education Agency Standards. Your students will:

- compare and order fractions using concrete and pictorial models;
- generate equivalent fractions;
- compare two fractional quantities in problem-solving situations using a variety of methods; and
- model and record addition and subtraction of fractions with like denominators in problem-solving situations.

ACTIVITIES FOR ADVANCED LEARNING SERIES

Camp Fraction
Solving Exciting Word Problems Using Fractions
Set around a trip to summer camp, students work with fractions in a problem-solving format, while learning a little history, trivia, and fun facts about a number of different items.
Grades 4–6 $11.95

Creative Writing
Using Fairy Tales to Enrich Writing Skills
Use fairy tales to challenge and motivate your students. This activity book contains fun reading and writing activities that pique students' interest in creative writing.
Grades 4–8 $11.95

Extra! Extra!
Advanced Reading and Writing Activities for Language Arts
The book includes standards-based independent language arts activities for students in grades K–2 such as developing a newspaper and inventing new words.
Grades K-2 $11.95

Math Problem Solvers
Using Word Problems to Enhance Mathematical Problem Solving Skills
The standards-based problem solving strategies addressed in this book include drawing a picture, looking for a pattern, guessing and checking, acting it out, making a table or list, and working backwards.
Grades 2–3 $11.95

Puzzled by Math!
Using Puzzles to Teach Math Skills
Puzzled by Math! offers a collection of mathematical equations, knowledge, and skills in puzzle form. Standards-based content addresses addition, subtraction, multiplication, division, fractions, decimals, and algebra. Thirty-five exciting and challenging puzzles are included, as well as suggestions for using the material for a classroom learning center.
Grades 3–7 $11.95

Survival on the Reef
Exploring Amazing Animals and the Ways They Adapt to Their Environment
This challenging activity book addresses many essential skills and knowledge contained in the National Science Teachers Association standards using activities focused on the exciting environment of a coral reef, its inhabitants, and the ways these inhabitants have adapted to their world.
Grades 2–3 $11.95

Writing Stretchers
15 Minute Activities to Enrich Writing Skills
Standards-based activities address the areas of reading, writing, vocabulary, content literacy, creativity, and thinking skills, giving students a chance to enrich their writing skills.
Grades 4–8 $11.95

For a complete listing of titles in this series, please visit our website at

http://www.prufrock.com

PRUFROCK
PRESS INC.™